Mom I'm Sorry

C. R. WRATH

Mom I'm Sorry. Copyright © C.R. Wrath. All Rights Reserved. Printed in The United States of America.

Anti-Piracy Warning: The unauthorized reproduction or distribution of a copyrighted work is illegal. Criminal copyright infringement, including infringement without monetary gain, is investigated by the FBI and Is punishable by up to five years in federal prison and a fine of $250,000.

All rights reserved. No part of this book may be used or reproduced in any manner whatsoever, including internet usage without written permission from the author.

Formatting by Lacey Impellizeri
www.laceyimpellizeri.com

ISBN: 9781093440102

Dedication

Mom this goes out to you.

This book is dedicated to you because even though all of this happened to me in my life,

You were my knight in shining armor.

None of this is your fault and if I didn't go through any of this,

I would not be this strong.

I hope you're proud,

Mom I made it through because of you.

Thank you.

C.R. Wrath

Undercove

Cry me the blanket that sheds into my false comfort,

    Of wanting to be held and loved.

        Blinded by the act of a makeshift smile,

            Wishing considerably, it would stay a while.

My hopes, my dreams swayed by the force of human kind,

    But degraded and washed while others stand alone.

        I'm swimming, I'm swimming my arms are giving out,

            Below sea level I meet my friend the shark.

HAUNTED

Disgust is my best friend...

In the Mirror, mists of your shadow, always with you.

A baby could laugh, an elephant could toot,

but you laugh at what you deserve.

"You're wanted, you're loved,

you have the world ahead of you."

I guess the world knows what's better for you.

If you're happy you smile, if sad, you frown.

But with disgust, I get the crown.

C.R. Wrath

Angels Touch

Falling down,

    Angels frown.

        Body thumping,

            Adrenaline pumping.

Sipping spit,

    Spasm fit.

        Might be close,

            I'll take a lick.

Mom I'm Sorry

I'M OK

You laugh,

Who cares?

You smile,

Who cares?

You graduate,

Who cares?

You bust your knee,

There they are.

Crack their back,

There they are!

Give up,

Where are they?

C.R. Wrath

Glory Be Told

Flourished mists and trees made clear

Light brings up and wiped out fear

Bring me sun bring me hope

Make my earth below me bloat

Light up the sky from high above

Let the mother give birth to the cub

Let our inspiration go through out

Never fearing for any doubt

Life, live, love, peace

Never leaving the falling leaf

Nurture it, give it air

Let it all be clean and fair

Feed the hunger and bring life

Never stop if things just look nice

Keep on going forever at end

Let everything mold till your hearts content.

SPIRIT OF THE EAGLE

Flapping my wings and chasing it all

I fly up high to see them prowl

I soar up high to watch and see

Knowing the only one in the sky is me

I am the eagle that soars up high

To be the guardian and to be in the sky

I watch you all so you can be

Guided in the path that the elders wanted thee

Pounding winds and forceful yells

Chanting all the stories to tell

The spirit of strength and wisdom too

I am the beast that lives within you…

C.R. Wrath

Wood Not Speak

Spin the needle and sew the thread

Wrap your arms and sew the head

Don't you see it through their eyes?!

Their helpless screams and endless cries

Face so cold and made of wax

Stack them all up by the packs

Don't you hear their endless cheers?!

Drowning in their sorrowed fears

Look and see just how still

Make a move and they will kill

Held up high and stood by strings

Crowded theater and maidens sing

Are you ready, bring forth the show?

Just look at them their also sewn

Are you crazy?! I'm not a toy!

Don't lie to me I am a real boy!!!

Mom I'm Sorry

WOLVES DON'T CRY

I cry for the longing to be in your arms

Tilting my head and embracing the charms

I snuggle up against your chest

Cuddling up to get the rest

Breaths quicken and turn to faints

Nothing can hold my heart's restraints

Sickles form and turn to dust

Melt the boulders I will and must

Inside I hunt for the beast inside

To show a weakness I haven't cried

I stand my ground and stomp my feet

My paws melt into the snow and sink

Because I know that inside, I am forever strong

It doesn't matter to me how long

I will not make the ice my grave

The only thing is fire I crave

Twist my soul and singe and melt

Go ahead and make my pelt

I will be forever alive

The heart within can never die

C.R. Wrath

You may try to break me down

And remove my subtle crown

I turn my head and wipe my tears

Embracing all of my darkest fears

I lift my head into this ice like hell and howl saying…

Wolves don't cry…

Hunger Be Fed

Heart to beat

Head to feet

Rage to be

Break me free!

Can't you see

it's killing me?

My words are still

Upon that hill…

Walk be gain

Do you tame?

Learn from that

I got your back!

Heed the pact

While intact.

Blood be yours

Now open the doors…

C.R. Wrath

WHEN I?

When I look at her, I feel like I'm unstoppable

When I hug her I feel a warmth that's unbelievable

When I kiss her I feel unbreakable

DREAMS DO COME TRUE

When your heart beats fast you know,

When you see her smile grow.

Even when she's happy or sad,

Then you can always make her glad.

Being there for her every need,

Even when you dance, she takes the lead.

When she whispers to you, "Will always be together!"

That's when you know she means forever.

To tell you the truth, I'm one of them,

Dashing over a mountain for her I've been.

All she needs to do is whistle,

Only for her I'd take the pistol.

There's a lot more I would love to say to the woman I love,

For her I would do anything and above.

So, till the next time I get to do,

Is the moment when I can finally say, "I love you."

C.R. Wrath

Caw of The Snow

Sometimes, I want to break free from the dream,

That eats away my very soul from existing.

But the moment I try to spread my wings to fly

My black wings get clipped and I fall back down again.

As I try to caw, my voice is tainted by the unending fickle laughs of the snow.

But one day, one day the snow will settle and my wings will grow,

so that I will be the crow that sings and flies the loudest.

UNSPOKEN

Death kiss my throat, kiss my neck,

Lick my back and taste the sweat.

In a haste vision blurry,

My life just in some hurry.

I feel numb, my memories, start speaking with a twisted tongue,

Puffing away hoping to choke a lung.

I pray with might my hands to my chest,

That god can still kiss my beaten chest.

Who is that, calling me with a forked tongue?

Rhyming in unison I lay life among.

Bless me father for I have sinned,

The sun it's burning my faith be skinned.

C.R. Wrath

Echoed the Macaw

Isn't it funny to watch people laugh?

To see how long one's life might last?

A second goes by and an eternity as well,

Finding my home, tucked a room in hell.

I remember when I could hear them sing,

The birds that chirped following that spring.

The Macaw used to echo, "Happy is brave,"

But who knew, the echo took to grave?

You'll Get There

"I'm a tree, give me water so I can grow."

If that's the case, I'll use a bucket.

C.R. Wrath

Sense of Harmony

The wind feels cold,

Mud feels moist.

The sun is shiny,

It's warm and can get hot.

Snow is so cold,

And when it melts turns into water.

What I would do to feel again.

WHEN'S THE TIME

There's a timeline,

Where do I fall?

In the beginning with four?

Or the end with two?

Who? What? When? Why?

Stop it. I said stop it!

Find out and go out there.

C.R. Wrath

Reality

No matter your age it's all the same,

a bottle when you're a baby, and until you're old.

Far Away

Moving on,

More and more.

I don't care,

I'm sorry.

My feelings were never important,

So, I'm sorry I don't care.

You look at me with eyes of innocence like it's your first time,

But I'm sorry, I don't care.

Not if I'm a used napkin thrown on the ground again,

Crumpled and used.

Apologies are no longer required,

And anger morphed to numbness.

Goodbye, and I don't care.

Planted Dreams

I want to go to Neverland forever,

Just never want to wake up again.

Mom I'm Sorry

DEAR ROMEO, FROM ROMEO

I don't have to save myself anymore,

No longer am I afraid of anything else.

Only thing to fear now, are my demons that pat my back,

and for this I say,

"Dear Romeo, if you find this, make sure I don't wake up."

C.R. Wrath

Mr. Butterfly

I popped out of my cocoon and sprouted into a full butterfly.

I found you later flying with Ms. Ladybug.

Together we were odd, however we came together in unison and made our own rhythm.

From day till night Mr. Butterfly, you were a role model, teaching me how to fly and to have fun.

You were always there...

But then Mr. Butterfly, you had to get sick...

Ladybug and I laid by you countless nights, holding your cold hands while you were unconscious because a child swatted your wing.

I fly by you, wishing you were OK, but you were unconscious for a while, but I stood by you, even though you warned me not to get close, Mr. Butterfly, but we both knew I never listened. You flew sideways, your wing was wrecked, but Ms. Ladybug helped you home.

I saw you and you weren't the same after that. You had a permanent paleness to you.

We may have fought, but we also, laughed and cried together, and from my hatching, till today, Mr. Butterfly, I never left you.

The screams you made when you got home until you went to bed, drinking through a straw because that's all you could muster, the pain you went through...

Mom I'm Sorry

Until the morning I flew with you until your eyes paused through time and you didn't breathe anymore.

Mr. Butterfly, I never wanted you to leave me,

Dad, I will always love you.

Fuck cancer.

C.R. Wrath

Fickle

Disappear into the night,

Spread my eyes to make me fright.

Please dear god, oh save my soul,

I'm trying, I'm trying to still stay whole.

Cover my ears, and seal my mouth,

Rip out my spine to make me slouch.

I gave my angel a blade to poke,

To grab my neck and slit my throat.

Why do you laugh? And watch me cry?

Faking a laugh and living a lie.

Can it end? Can it stop? So it can be real?

It's weird to say, but I want to feel.

BE STILL

I used to love, and smile upon amends,

Fingers counting, waiting to join the dead.

My eyes are black, and spirit of dark,

My inner child roughly fed to shark.

Swim away, fouled angered beast,

It's OK to take your feast.

Dawn has broken and fled to dawn,

This life bores me, instead I yawn.

C.R. Wrath

Finished

End me now,

Finish my soul,

Cripple my mind,

Cup half full.

Leg is hurt,

From deepening cuts,

World is crying,

Unfed pups.

It's sad,

It hurts,

The unfinished vow,

Until you die,

But please, end me now.

CIRCLE

Liar,

Thief,

Blood,

Ouch,

Pain,

Finished,

Hurt,

Begin.

C.R. Wrath

HIGH FIVE:

Are you OK?

Is Everything Fine?

What's been new?

Hey?

Hi?

You Around?

Lol?

Anything up?

Ttyl?

Um?

OK?

....

..

.

All it took was once sentence to finally snap the alligators mind.

SULKED LULLABY

I keep telling the model to move,

Instructing them to pose a certain way.

"Stop it! Not like that, this way!"

They don't get it,

But I do!

So why aren't they listening to me?

My head is clear I promise it is!

OK I see your point.

Stop laughing at me.

C.R. Wrath

BABY LET OUT

I don't know what I want anymore,

And sometimes the answer's right there.

It scares me though, the truth of who I will become, or be.

I no longer need a push, sometimes, it's all about excepting it.

Even if you don't want to.

Mom I'm Sorry

MIRROR YOUR THOUGHTS

This will be the last time I tell you,

Stop degrading me.

I'm nothing like you,

Nor do I care what you become,

Or even what happens to you.

You're a liar, you're a fool,

you're a broken glassed fake reflection.

It took me a long time to see that in you,

And for that I am the fool.

Make no mistake though a fool can learn,

To never trust a human being again.

Congratulations to you.

I'm Human So Are You

Whore,

Fag,

Slut,

Freak,

Animal,

Words to describe me?

I'm human, we aren't different. We are the same.

PEELED FLESH

"If I forget it, then it must not be important."

What if the pain is unbearable, I just don't want to remember?

C.R. Wrath

REALITY

I'm a virgin to living,

It gets hard.

Wishing for my mother to tuck me in at night still.

It gets dark in my head sometimes, my skin feeling so cold.

"It's fine! You'll be OK," is what I'm told.

I want to wake up again at 6a.m to watch morning cartoons with not a worry.

But it's 8a.m and work just called, now life is in a hurry.

LIFE TRUTH

I might be loose,

That still doesn't give you the right to fuck me in life.

NOTICE

For a brief second, I felt it,

I was happy.

Shattered

My fault?

Self-cult.

Self-help,

Loathed Yelp.

Because in my chest I hate my heart,

Everyone says, you don't know art.

To them I say go burn in hell.

Don't let your ass fall,

Because the devil and I don't kill and tell…

C.R. Wrath

Checked Out

My eyes are cold,

My skin is rough.

My veins are old,

My mind is fluff.

My head is blank,

My tongue is pale.

Body be planked,

My life be jail.

BURST

Grab my throat,

Lick my sweat.

Bang my head against the wall!

Strangle my wrists with a kiss,

Making me beg your name.

C.R. Wrath

Goodbye

I'm hanging off of a hill,

The view, it worries me.

I can feel my pulse in my wrists,

The problem is I'm not scared...

I'm ready to jump.

WOW

Don't leave me alone with my thoughts,

They're not safe.

C.R. Wrath

Stop It, Please

Get out of my head,

Enough with your lies.

Damn it, leave me alone!

The voices aren't calm,

They're roaring.

I touch something, or I smell something, I remember the pain.

Go away, [As I say Crying.] I don't want you here!

So why are you still? Then I remember, you never will...

Even if I ask you.

Mom I'm Sorry

GONE

Please

   Let

      Me

         Go...

            P = Pressure

            L = Lonely

            E = Erased

            A = Angered

            S = Silenced

            E = Eager

                  L = Left

                  E = End

                  T = Tired

                        M = Moron

                        E = Effortless

                              G = Gone

                              O = Over

C.R. Wrath

Worry No More

Run away with me,

To a place where there's no more worries.

A place where everyone is at peace with one another,

And all you see are flowers covering the ground.

When I got there,

We finally arrived at the graveyard

And the tombstone had my name on it.

MIND CRUNCH

I'm fevered, induced in my skull.

I can feel the crack, in my head, a splinter.

Snap open my chest and take out my heart of black and spit on it for me.

I know it's deserved and it would bring me to peace.

Disgusting,

Vile,

There's no more truth that can be seen because the light in the tunnel was really a flashlight,

Held by god waving it in his toy playground.

C.R. Wrath

Spoken

I never wrote a note saying goodbye,

Or told everybody I loved them.

The laughs and hugs were always special to me,

and none of it was your fault.

Mom I'm Sorry

TORTURE

I can't anymore,

I'm done,

I hate you,

I hate myself,

I don't want this gift of life.

Give it to someone who will treasure it, it's too much for me.

Between the Lines

Leave me alone!

                                                                       [Please don't]

I can't take this anymore!

                                                                       [Just hug me]

I want to die!

                                                                       [Just hold me tighter]

Goodbye...

                                                                       [Don't leave me]

WANTED

A bow for a girl,

A gun for a boy.

Give a gun to a girl,

And a bow to a boy

and the world crumbles.

People's opinions and views will always change,

so why start caring?

Always be you, because you are special.

C.R. Wrath

Honest Friend

Today I met somebody like-minded,

It's a rare breed to honestly say that.

But it's a good feeling because then you realize,

You're not the only one in this world.

Mom I'm Sorry

JUST BREATHE

How can I calm down while you scream at me saying, "Stop overreacting!"

Why not ask me what's wrong?

C.R. Wrath

Never Forget Wings

Setting the scene: I'm eight years old and in bed.

I'm being read Peter Pan to go to bed.

I'm kissed on the head to go to sleep and I hear a voice sing me to sleep.

Damn... I woke up from my sleep and reality hit me. I'm 24, living at home, everything has changed except one thing.

Peter, I still believe in fairies. Bangarang!

BE STRONG

I can't forget the times...

The time I got slapped around,

Screamed in my face,

My face shoved low,

Or the time the lady almost drowned me.

Being young and choked out, thrown in the street,

Or my tiny head bashed against the wall.

More has happened in my life, however, what's the fun with saying it all in one poem?

I use these as an example, I will never forget what you all did to me, but I forgive you.

Forgiveness makes you a stronger person, I will never forget what you did, but I forgive you.

C.R. Wrath

Hilarity Of Pain

My mind's on fire,

My head is spurting.

Eyes of evil my tongue,

Is flirting.

Feed me now my tears of math,

Forever unspoken my pains I laugh.

HESITANT

I feel like my tears are blood drowning my spit,

Choking the life out of me.

C.R. Wrath

Darling Dream

When life gets tough,

I'm no longer here.

Why?

Because in my head I entered a new world.

One that I made where I'm important,

the setting always changes, but I mean something.

Mom I'm Sorry

YOU NEED TO HEAR THIS

Get yourself through the day,

Turn your customers into dragons,

Your boss is the goblin king,

And you're the hero.

Slay them all and remember how proud I am of you.

C.R. Wrath

NEVER

When you lay your head down to sleep at night,

Please, don't forget me.

I don't want to be forgotten.

Mom I'm Sorry

CHOCOLATE

Maybe it's the way he looks at me,

Or rubs my arms.

Could it possibly be him speaking my name?

I guess the subtle charms.

Whatever it may be, I come to say,

That I hope we can meet again one day.

Through all the mountains and all the birds,

I come across you with the start of, "Hey."

C.R. Wrath

DEAR QUEER

Tell me one more painful joke,

Fake laugh louder to the croak.

My closet door fell, why not yours?

Fault be mine, loving mine mores?

Mom I'm Sorry

I Say Let's Fly

Right into the dreamless sky,

Spread my wings and try to fly.

Overhearing perfect lies,

Clip my wings and let me die.

C.R. Wrath

Bros_

I know you need me, but I'm not here for even myself.

I love you the most,

You're my best friend but know when you suffer, I suffer ten times more.

Knowing that I should have and wanted to be there for you,

But never are you ever alone.

Mom I'm Sorry

JUST LET ME FLY

Flying is the mental thought of a beautiful lie,

Like, if I jump, I'll be able to sprout wings,

Take a breath,

And smell the fresh air when, in reality, I know I'll splat

But please, I'm begging you, give me the lie.

C.R. Wrath

Fool

The shouting is louder with you breathing in my ear!

Back away, my tingled fear.

My heart is pounding, my hands are sweat,

If I turned around, you'd stab me I bet.

Can't trust, can't rely, not a simple truth,

Beating the work I do, destroying my youth.

TOO LATE

Can you go?

Far away so I can't see?

Can you run?

Faster than a breath in one?

Shut up please, every word you say is a lie!

The answer is no, I will not trust you.

Go away.

C.R. Wrath

POUNDING

You are poison on my tongue,

My sweat and desire.

My fist clenches to the thought of me having you.

My legs wiggle as I lick my sweat from brow,

Because I know my thoughts are unending of you.

You Will Be OK

My head needs a break from all of this.

I see a car and as it's about to pass me full speed I jump in front of it. [In my mind.]

The trolley goes by and I hear the squealing as it comes closer, I fall underneath it. [In my mind.]

I'm up high on a bridge and I jump off it, landing on a passing car down below. [In my mind.]

These lines are fading.

C.R. Wrath

Relax

Where I live in mind, demons cry for me,

As I cry for the innocent who need help.

I am no saint, nor am I claiming to.

However, the thing I desire most is peace.

WILLING TO CHANGE

I'm fighting to be fine,

And drowning in my thoughts.

My clouded head is crusting,

I work too much,

I'm trying to be a better brother and lover.

But will I ever be there?

Seriously

You liar, can you leave me alone because I'm done with you?

Forever this time.

STAY AWAY

It's better sometimes to keep a distance from people for the sake of saving your feelings.

I grew up with what I thought would be my best friend, who turned into my brother.

Where did he go?

He left me forever.

I grew attached to my band teacher who, if I had any questions, answered with a smile on his face.

He died.

My closer friend? Raped and hit by a car.

I met a family and within 24 hours the family burnt down with the home.

So, when people say maybe it's better that I keep you at a distance,

Or somebody might not respond to your "hi."

Don't get offended, sometimes it's better that you never knew us.

C.R. Wrath

THIS FAR APART

I go to work all day,

To come home and prove I'm a man.

It gets tiring because mentally you question if you want to be a man anymore.

The world on your shoulders and everyone looks at you to make their life better.

I will say this one time.

Do not rely on me for everything,

I know I can do it,

But you are not worth my health.

Mom I'm Sorry

I'M WITH YOU

Its intimate living,

You get to know yourself,

And with the cold reality that you are your best friend.

It looks like it's time to date yourself again and get to know you.

Man, women, whoever you are.

You're beautiful and I love you for who you are.

C.R. Wrath

YOU ARE PERFECT

Life can be 1134,

But sometimes we need to dance with demons.

Mom I'm Sorry

ONE DAY

I can't forgive my Dad for dying,

It wasn't his fault.

But I can't forgive him for leaving this time.

C.R. Wrath

The Four Reasons

I will give you the reasons why I hate you.

    1. You lied to me.

    2. You betrayed me.

    3. Made me think it was my fault.

    4. You went away without saying goodbye.

You Won't be Far

I look at you and envy, knowing I will never be with you.

C.R. Wrath

SERPENT

In front of me you like me,

Behind me you hate me.

In front of me you laugh to me,

Behind me you cry.

In front of me you claim to know,

Behind me you question.

In front of me, you say were friends,

Behind me, you talk about me.

You're done. Get out of my life.

COME CLOSER

Do not expect for me to ask how you're doing

if I see you sad.

Do not expect for me to pretend to be happy

when you are sad.

Do not expect for me to not kiss your wounds

if I see you're hurt.

Do not think I'm going to turn my shoulder if I see you

want to talk about your day.

You will be disappointed.

Employee

E- Empty

M- Moldy

P- Painful

L- Lost

O- Once

Y- Yelled

E- Exit

E- Endured

DRIVE

Some days my glass is half full, others it's half empty.

Another saying that means nothing to me,

I just want to live my life the best that I can while giving it my all.

C.R. Wrath

CROWED THE COW

You respect me,

yet you talk to me like I'm five.

You tell me I'm a leader

except you "manage" the things I know I'm good at.

You are seriously worthless.

Why not change yourself,

so you can change the people that you work with.

That's leadership.

TURN YOUR EYE

In my time if need where are you?

When I fall did you help me up?

You laughed and told me I couldn't do it!

I'm not rubbing it in your face,

I'm bigger than that,

All I'm saying is I'm sorry for you.

C.R. Wrath

Depends

Other days I want to destroy the world

and laugh at the tears of my enemies.

Some days I want to cuddle and eat cupcakes.

#BEYOU

I sing a tune, to bleach your name,

To re-write history with no to blame.

Music is power, raw soul to build.

Love, desire, and violence is stilled.

We change people's minds, that's the power of it all.

Lyrics and writings are all without a flaw.

#beyou

C.R. Wrath

I Do

Through my eyes I feel you,

Every memory and nightmare we share now.

That's what happens when we said I do.

Your fears,

Nightmares,

Strengths and weaknesses, all of it is beautiful,

And I want you.

Mom I'm Sorry

RUDE

If you interrupt a customer service worker,

You like to cut off their sales pitch when they are trying because you,

"Heard it before."

You are the problem and reason why,

"Customers not always right."

Reflect

To the lady that called me an idiot and said I was the reason that ruined her day because she waited in line for six minutes,

I hope your day gets better because obviously there's something going on.

Feel better soon.

I hope you're not like that forever.

Mom I'm Sorry

BE REAL

Every day is worth a smile.

C.R. Wrath

BOTH SIDES

"Don't judge a book by its cover?"

Sometimes we need to, in order to understand their true intent.

Exquisite

Damn,

I can't stop looking at the way you walk,

The way you talk.

You carry yourself like a woman.

C.R. Wrath

Every Little Thing

You, that one person who gave me a compliment today

and told me, "I was gorgeous."

Thank you for making my day.

REAL

One day you will be tested

and your deepest desire or sin will surface.

When it does,

Remember you are only human.

C.R. Wrath

Remember

You did hurt me,

You will pay.

LADYBUG

I never claimed to be the hero, however, what I do have is words.

Most powerful things we have that can make or break someone.

With my words you deserve to hear this.

"Mom, you are my hero and thank you for the ladybugs."

C.R. Wrath

STRENGTH

Sometimes when I look out at the rain, I can see the upside-down splash.

Reversing time for even a second while, I remember the memories of when I

Was in a diaper painting on myself waiting for your white car. You went out to work.

Mom, I never did leave the door until you came back home.

I still am there at the door in my head Mom.

I'm proud of you.

Mom I'm Sorry

MR. MOM

You raised me single and all,

Gave me a push as I lay and fall.

You did me good, you did me right,

You gave me my lion in heart to fight.

I cry, I pray till night and day,

I made you proud from May to May.

My rock, my warrior, my single Mom,

Always remember I think you're bomb.

C.R. Wrath

STARVING

I eat when I'm sad,

I eat when I'm mad.

I draw when I'm happy,

I eat when I'm crappy.

I laugh here and there,

This pain I can't bear.

Smack the fork away from me,

So I can have no more obesity.

WATCH YOURSELF

You spoiled ass silver spooned brat.

Look at me when you complain about your life and issues.

I've given you the shirt on my back on a rainy day,

And a hand in need to erase your pain.

I hand you the key to my chest.

Thank you for stealing everything precious to me.

I won't trust you again.

C.R. Wrath

Tough Love

Believing it's possible is all you need to succeed.

Will you stay at home every day keep saying, "That idea will always be there?"

Or

"Tomorrow's when I will start?"

That's not believing, those words aren't inspiring.

Be proud of yourself, believe in you.

If you scoff and say that's impossible, you're wrong.

You don't want to hear that, but you're wrong.

Own it, and make that change, because I'm proud of you.

"Who knows, maybe this is what I needed to tell myself when I was younger,

But I'm passing this on to you."

Mom I'm Sorry

REALIZE IN YOU

You're strange,

You're crazy,

I don't get you,

I think you're weird,

Silly,

Deranged,

Insane,

And out there.

That means you're special.

C.R. Wrath

Final Words

I will attempt to love you,

But please don't bite me again.

WAKE UP

You ignorant, selfish goof,

Stop raising your kids to be self-entitled.

I see grandparents eating with their grandkids but not mentally there,

But on their phone.

I bumped into a mom eating out with her kids, the nine-year-old looking child was on his tablet.

What is your child's favorite TV show? What does he/she like to do as a hobby the most?

Do you get to know them more? Participate in their hobbies?

"You don't understand I work,"

"They're getting older now!"

"They would be better if they grew up!"

I guess you grew up then to.

Do you feel better not knowing your kids and keeping that distance between you?

Make that change because they love you and want you.

C.R. Wrath

INNER SELF

I'm trying to catch my breath

as I fall down in the cold puddled street.

My fingers are numb and I'm reaching for food.

I cough and I taste iron in my throat as I'm kicked in the face.

I know I'll get warm, I just got to hang on a little longer.

Mom I'm Sorry

NO MORE H8

S- Sensitive

L- Loving

U- United

T- Tolerant

#stoptheh8

U- Understanding

G- Grateful

L -Laughter

Y- Yourself

F- Fun

A- Amazing

G- Great

G- Giving

O- Oath

T- Thoughtful

C.R. Wrath

Every Word

This message is for you if you need me right now,

You're not alone,

You're not ugly, or unattractive.

I think you're enough.

You gave it your all today.

That's enough for me.

You did it kid.

I will always be there for you,

Every word is a hug from me to you.

EARTHED

Behind the sunny petal is wilted,

And soil with flooded acid.

Give me the water & sun I need to sprout.

C.R. Wrath

THROTTLE

I'm pushing harder on the throttle.

It's black outside I can't see anything.

You feel it with me?

Your pulse rapidly racing, not being able to control your grip,

And your body's about to burst?

Slow down.

Mom I'm Sorry

WHERE ARE YOU?

Some days holding the cross it's kissed.

Other days it's sworn at and thrown under my pillow.

C.R. Wrath

Move On

You grabbed my neck and slapped my face.

Wished me dead without a trace.

Attempted the drown behold I'm true,

No matter what you did,

I love you.

Mom I'm Sorry

POLAROID

Look back at our pictures,

We did so much together.

Let's buy more frames.

C.R. Wrath

Kind

I gave you a black rose,

You gave me your wishes and thoughts

So we can drink the purity of forever.

Mom I'm Sorry

GET UP

Legs are rotting holding you up for too long,

Will you help yourself?

C.R. Wrath

You And I

I'm going to die one day,

Hopefully my words touched you.

Seasonal

Each holiday brings smiles and tears,

Smiles for the memories I have for you.

Tears for knowing you're not there.

C.R. Wrath

LOOK AGAIN

LOSE = S.O.E.L

Mom I'm Sorry

THINKER

It's gross in this tight room,

Being clumped and confined in this small space.

My feet hang outside the bed, there's not enough room to scream.

It's too dusty.

C.R. Wrath

Thirsty

Pour me a glass of water,

It's been a hot day and my feet hurt,

My back aching,

And sweat is staining my clothes.

Write a letter shouting,

Bursting an eardrum surrounding the

Thesaurus of my mind.

CLOSE

We went to elementary school and played until the sun welcomed us.

Running away to the world of Zorn where us, the wizards, we both needed to escape.

Where did you go? Why did you disappear?

You weren't a nobody to me.

You existed.

ONE WHISPER

You will never fully trust someone,

Until a secret is shared between one another.

Something I've never shared with anybody

Is this,

"Phones scare me,

horrible memories are attached to them."

I trust you with my secret now.

STRINGS

Every day is a new mask.

The mask of a brother,

A son,

And a man.

Face resting in rotting decay peeling off the

Theatrical play of an exhausted host.

C.R. Wrath

Beauty Hurts

Thorns never hide themselves to you.

Come close to them and blood mixes with the stem's core.

People are harder to understand.

Mom I'm Sorry

REDO

I want to go back in time,

Before I met you.

But this time,

I won't say hi.

C.R. Wrath

BE MY DRUG

Sitting on a grass hill,

I see you.

Capturing your beauty with a pencil,

Replicating that smile that takes the breath away from my lungs,

But it's impossible to capture the full perfection of you.

You're my heroin.

Mom I'm Sorry

BUZZ

Today was a rough day,

I think about the horror,

The yelling,

The negative.

I want to end it all.

[Phone buzzes, I get a text.]

"Just letting you know how special you are."

You made the sadness go away.

C.R. Wrath

Aquarium Dream

This aquarium is gigantic.

There's a golden statue in front of two stingrays

About to bite each other's tails.

With a ring of gold slanted around them,

I go to the glass and murky water.

The tank is deep and there's no bottom and in the distance a black dot with fins still.

I turn my head for a second

And back.

The creature's chestnut eye looks at me as I look back at it.

We got something from each other with one look.

Envy of it wanting to get out of its tank,

And I wanting to go back in.

Mom I'm Sorry

PUSH

Your body wants to give up,

But do you?

C.R. Wrath

SELF-LOSS

I lost my mind years ago, now I'm picking scars.

Acknowledgments:

Mom, family, fellow author J.M. Fejeran, editor Joseph Arc, cover artist Omtay, and dear friends.

You all supported me and I thank you for that.

Hopefully my experiences in life encourage people that living is the better option and that you are not Alone in this world.

You, dear reader, you're beautiful and I love you and whatever you're going through remember you are Not alone,

Even though we feel like we are.

Mary,

You are a Shooting Star.

Never forget to Shine.

— C.R. Wrath